Bizarre Creatures

Tamim Ansary

Illustrations by Derrick Williams

1   2   3   4   5   6   7   8   9   10

ISBN 0-8250-4967-3

Copyright © 2004

Walch Publishing

P. O. Box 658 • Portland, Maine 04104-0658

walch.com

Printed in the United States of America

Bizarre Creatures

Table of Contents

Introduction

There are many things for people to fear in this world. Car accidents, for example, kill thousands of people every year. The flu once wiped out millions worldwide. Lightning often strikes people during thunderstorms.

Yet, somehow, no one gets goose bumps over cars or bad weather or the flu season. We save our deepest shivers for things we can't even see. We fear the dark and "things that go bump in the night."

And all over the world, people turn fear of this type into stories. They make up monsters to explain the fears that make no sense. You may have shivered over such stories yourself. Perhaps you have heard tales of witches, ghosts, or werewolves. People in other places have their own monsters. Africans and Asians, for example, tell stories most Americans have never heard. Even in this country, different groups have different monster tales.

Get ready to meet six monsters from different lands. Compare them to monsters you have heard about. See if you think they are more scary or less so. Which ones would make good movies or television shows? Why or why not?

Shapeshifters of the Muslim World

There's a feeling you may get sometimes when you're alone in the dark. You may get it in a deserted graveyard, too, under a full moon. Or try spending a night in a damp basement. You are almost sure to get the feeling there. What you feel is fear when there is nothing to fear. The hair stands up on the back of your neck. You get a weird feeling between your shoulders. All these signs may be telling you a *jinn* is near.

What are jinns? To understand fully, you have to travel in the Middle East or Central Asia. Many people there believe in jinns. They will tell you jinns are a whole race of unpleasant creatures. They share the earth with us. Jinns have no one shape or form. In fact, much of the time they have no form at all. You can't see them. You can only feel them in your bones, heart, and hair. That's because jinns have a habit of getting inside other creatures.

Jinns don't slip into people all that much. They spend most of their time inside animals. The animal they most often "drive" is a cat. They like gray cats best, but any cat will do. There is one way to tell if a cat is really a jinn:

Offer it some catnip. If it takes no interest in the weed, it is probably a jinn. So say those who believe in jinns.

Sometimes jinns take a shape that people can see. We know this because some people have seen them, or at least they say they have. Such stories are quite common in parts of Asia. Here is one such story, told by a man named Shahbuddin.

Shahbuddin lived in the city of Kabul, Afghanistan. He owned a used clothing store. Most of his family lived in a village near the city. In Afghanistan, people get Fridays off and work only until noon on Thursdays. So on Thursdays, Shahbuddin often rode his bicycle home to his village.

It was a long ride—about 10 miles. There was no real road to the village, only a dirt path. This path ran among bare hills. There were no houses to be seen along the way.

Shahbuddin usually set off at about 2:00 or 3:00 in the afternoon. In the summer, he could make it to the village before dark. But his jinn story took place in late fall. That Thursday, he got a late start because he ran into a friend. They went to a tea house for a few hours. The sun was sinking by the time Shahbuddin took off.

Dusk fell before he even got out of the

city. He rode on. After a while the moon came up, but it was a new moon. It did not give off much light. Shahbuddin had a light on his bicycle, but the power came from his back wheel. As long as he kept moving, his light kept shining. If he stopped, the light went out.

About three miles from the village, Shahbuddin came around a corner. He saw the ruin of an old mill. Shahbuddin was thirsty. He knew there was a stream behind the mill, so he stopped for a drink. As soon as he stopped, his light went out. So he climbed down the hillside in the dark.

Something flitted away.

He thought it was a wild animal, such as a fox. He made his way to the mill and peeked around the corner. There he could just make out a strange sight. A giant lay on his back. He looked dead. He was probably about as long as three city buses. Crawling all over him was a crowd of small men. They were not much bigger than cats. They looked very busy. Shahbuddin did not know what they were doing, and he did not try to find out. He ran back to the path, jumped on his bicycle, and sped away.

Later, he told his family and friends what he had seen. Someone told him that a lot of wild cats lived near that mill. But Shahbuddin always believed he had seen jinns that night.

Jinns show up as characters in Arabian fairy tales. They have magical powers. They can make people's wishes come true. Many of these stories have been translated into English. They are found in a book called *The Arabian Nights.* In English, the jinns are called "genies." You may have seen genies in movies such as *Aladdin.* These genies are often friendly, lovable, and lots of fun.

But in the Middle East, no one thinks of jinns as fun. They know that jinns can slip into a person's body. They can use a person like a car. People who believe in jinns know how this feels—awful. They have seen people with jinns inside them. The people scream, shake, and jump around. It is not a pretty sight.

There is a creature in the United States that is somewhat like a jinn. Even its name sounds similar. It is the *chindri*.

You might run into stories about this creature in the Southwest. The Navajo people believe in it. They believe that chindris are created to punish people who have done something wrong. Powerful medicine men can "sing" them into being. Those who have been good need not worry. A medicine man could not call up a chindri to go after them, even if he wanted to. Those who have been bad, however, may be in very deep trouble indeed.

Like a jinn, a chindri can take any form or shape. It can do this because it gets inside other living things. The Navajo say that if an animal's eyes look dead, it may be a chindri. If its eyes do not reflect light, it may be a chindri. If an animal is doing something strange at night, it is probably a chindri. For example, one man saw a coyote walking on its hind legs. That was almost surely a chindri.

Once a chindri has been born, it cannot be killed until its work is done. Bullets kill only the animal that is carrying the chindri. The chindri itself does not die. It just leaves the dying animal the way air leaves a balloon. The chindri then goes into another beast. And it keeps doing this until its work is done.

The sad story of the Long Salt family is one example. The story began in 1825.

The Long Salts were a big Navajo family of over a hundred people. One of the family members got sick, and a blind old medicine man was called in. He said the family had to pay him with the meat of five sheep for his help. Two men were told to get the meat, but they decided to cheat the old man. They brought him antelope meat instead of sheep. They figured the blind man would never know the difference.

But he did know. And when he got home, he sang for a chindri. A few weeks later, members of the Long Salt family began to die. The family called a meeting. They quickly figured out that a chindri was hunting them down. They did not know why, however. What wrong had they done?

The two cheaters then spoke up and admitted their crime. The family was horrified. A few of them went to talk to the medicine man. They told him that only two of the family had done wrong. No one else was in on it. Why should the whole family suffer?

The old man said he would think about it for ten days. Then he would decide what he should do about the chindri. Sadly, he died before the ten days were up. He never had a chance to call off the chindri. By the end of that week, two more members of the Long Salt family had fallen ill. The chindri was still after them, and now no one could call it off.

In the years that followed, the Long Salts all died young. Some of them married and had children. But none of them lived past their early twenties. The family kept shrinking.

In 1925, a man named John Winslow

 met the last of the Long Salts. She was a teenager named Alice. Her mother had died when she was seven. Her father had passed away when she was nine.

After the last of her family died, she became listless. An old Navajo medicine man named Hosteen Behegade took her in. He cared for her as if she were his own daughter. He tried his best to keep her safe. He got other medicine men to help sing for her. But Alice grew ever weaker.

Behegade started to move Alice around. He was hoping to stay ahead of the chindri. He tried to make sure they never spent two nights in the same place.

But in 1928, a blizzard caught Behegade and Alice on the plains. They had to stay in the same hut for a few nights in a row. The storm kept raging. Behegade thought the snow would keep them safe. He thought no animal could go out in weather like that. And yet, on the third night, Behegade heard an owl cry outside. He knew it meant the end had come.

In the morning, sure enough, Alice was dead. That chindri had finished its job, and it was never heard from again.

The Half Men of Africa

Do you ever get the feeling that someone is following you? Often it's a feeling you get between your shoulder blades. It might happen to you on a dark street or in the woods. You want to laugh and tell yourself it's just a feeling. But then you hear a sound.

Or do you? You stop and turn. No one is there.

You start walking again. But right away, you hear it again. Footsteps? Or just leaves rustling in the wind? Again you turn. Again you see no one.

In America, people call this feeling paranoia. It's all in your head, they say. In parts of Africa, people have another explanation. Someone really *is* following you, they say. It's one of the Half Men.

The Half Men of Africa

Different tribes know this fellow by different names. The Zulu call him Tikdoshe. To the Kohekohe, farther north, he is Hai Uru. In the Republic of the Congo, people know him as Adroa.

He's the same fellow, though. You can tell by his most striking feature. He has only half a body. He has one arm, one leg, and one eye. If he had both halves he would look like a normal person—but he doesn't.

The Half Man following you is probably one of the thin ones. This type of Half Man is so thin, he has only a front and a back. When he turns sideways, he can't be seen. Each time you look back, the Half Man turns sideways. That's why you can't see him.

Most of the time, he just follows at a distance. All he wants to do is watch you. Some even say the Half Men look out for people. They tell stories of a Half Man guiding a lost traveler home. There is only one problem with getting such help. You may never tell anyone about it. If you do, you may lose the ability to speak at all.

The Half Men of Africa

Some people say the Half Man has scarier ways. They say his mood changes if he gets close to you. To be blunt—this creature feeds on people. He will eat other things, too—frogs, toads, insects, or whatever he can catch. But he enjoys human flesh the most. There is only one way to escape from him. Just keep walking at your normal pace. Don't look around. Don't start running. If you turn, that Half Man will be all over you.

Then you're in for a fight! If the Half Man pins you, he eats you. That's the bad news. But there's good news, too. If you win, the Half Man gives you certain magic powers. He may show you plants that can heal any illness. He may give you the power to defeat your enemies.

Some say there is only one Half Man. He haunts lonely places in the forest, carrying an ax. According to the stories, this grim fellow was born of a spiteful woman. Her husband had two wives. The first wife was jealous of the second one. She tricked her co-wife into throwing away her own baby. The trick backfired. Everyone felt sorry for the mother who had lost her baby. They brought her rich gifts. A few days later, she found her baby. Then she had rich gifts and her baby as well.

When the jealous woman saw this, she threw her own baby into the river. But no one sympathized with her. No one brought her any gifts. In the end, she had to get her child back from the river. By then, he had only half a body.

Still others say the Half Man is not alone. He has a wife, a Half Woman. Together, they have a child, a Half Boy. They live in a village of Half People.

These one-legged, one-armed, one-eyed villagers can fly. Their huts are made of elephants' tusks and python skins. They have pots of honey and stores of meat and fat. Don't ask where they get the meat. In fact, you would be wise to avoid this village. The trouble is, the village is invisible to human eyes. You never know when you're near it—or in it.

An African named Aaron Mwabaya says there is one sure sign of a Half Man in your area. You see the print of a single human foot next to a hyena's. The hyena is the Half Man's pet. Of course this tip won't help in America. Here, there are no hyenas. If Half Men live in America, one of them may start following you at any time. You'll know by that feeling between your shoulder blades. If you ever get that feeling, just remember—Don't look back!

What does a vampire look like? Many people would say he's a suave fellow who wears a cape and talks with an accent. He goes to elegant parties at night. By day, he sleeps in a coffin.

But this only describes the most famous vampire—Count Dracula. His legend comes from Romania, a country in Eastern Europe. Other countries have vampire legends of their own. The oldest one comes from ancient China. This vampire is called *kiang shi*. Stories about him were told over 2,000 years ago.

The newest version comes from Puerto Rico. Here, people whisper about El Chupacabra. The name means "goatsucker." This vampire differs from all the others. How so? The name tells it all. El Chupacabra doesn't attack humans. It attacks barnyard animals. Sometimes it may suck the blood out of a cow, a goose, or a chicken. But mostly it prefers goats.

The legend of El Chupacabra got started around 1975. That year an odd thing started happening in Puerto Rico. Every once in a while, some farm animal died for no reason. At first, it seemed to have no wounds. Then, two small holes would be found on its neck or head. In every such case, the body was drained of blood. Not a single drop remained.

One of the first attacks occurred in the town of Moco. Some people later said they saw strange lights in the sky that night. An elderly blind woman lived next to the field where the attack happened. She said she couldn't sleep that night because of the noise. Hour after hour, the dogs kept barking. They kept running through the fields. The next morning, the farmer found his white cow in the field. It was dead and drained of blood. Yet, no blood had been spilled. That cow's white hide looked as spotless as fresh snow.

The next weird thing happened in San
Juan. This is the biggest city in Puerto
Rico. A television crew was shooting a
commercial. They wanted to film a perfect
sunrise. So they set up their movie
cameras on top of a tall building. They
pointed the cameras at the spot where the
sun would rise. They felt no need to stay
awake. They left the cameras running and
went to bed.

The next day, they played their film.
They had to gasp. A weird creature
walked briefly across the screen. It had
long ears, spikes on its back, and an evil
look. One of the men nearly fainted. The
others ran the tape backward to look at it

again. No one had ever seen such a creature before. Someone said, "Maybe that's . . . El Chupacabra—the goatsucker."

The name stuck. Soon more reports came trickling in. One farmer reported seeing El Chupacabra up close. He said he woke up one night to hear his chickens squawking. He thought a wild dog must have gotten into their coop. He grabbed his shotgun and hurried outside, barefoot. The full moon gave him a good view of the fields. He jogged to the chicken coop and flung the door open.

There stood El Chupacabra, with a chicken in each hand. It looked about 4 feet tall. Along its back ran quills like a porcupine's. It had scaly skin, big legs, and thin arms. Both its arms and its legs ended in claws. The creature glared at the farmer with huge, red eyes. Then it dropped the chickens and screeched. That frightening sound drove the farmer backward out of the yard. El Chupacabra bounded past him like a kangaroo. In one jump, it got onto a rooftop. There, it spread its bat-like wings and flew into the night.

Is there really such a creature? The answer is not clear. Creatures that fit this description have been seen before in history. They were statues, however, called gargoyles. People made such statues in the Middle Ages. They mounted gargoyles to church corners to scare away demons.

Did people of that time base gargoyles on a creature they had really seen?

Maybe.

On the other hand, just the opposite may be true. People of today may have seen pictures of gargoyles. They may be basing their descriptions of El Chupacabra on those pictures.

Maybe.

Just to be on the safe side, though, Puerto Rican farmers lock up their goats at night.

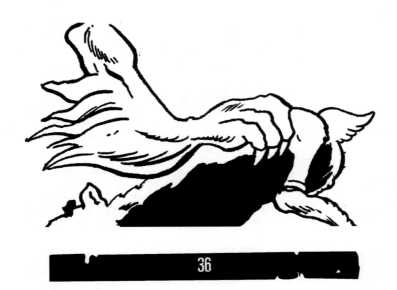

Have you ever heard the phrase, "screaming like a banshee!"? To most people nowadays, it is just an expression.

But where does it come from? Who are banshees, and why do they scream?

The Irish know. The legend of the banshees comes from their land. The Irish will tell you banshees are tall, thin women with long, streaming hair. You will sometimes see one crouching outside a family's front door. You might catch a glimpse of one peeping through the window at night. Most often, however, people come upon banshees in lonely outdoor places. They might spot one sitting by a stream. She is wearing a long gray skirt and a green shawl. Almost always, she is washing bundles of blood-soaked clothing. She might be old and wrinkled, but that is rare. Usually, a banshee is young and beautiful—except for her fiery red eyes.

What really marks a banshee, however, is the sound she makes. This sound ranges from humming to singing to wailing. And then there is that terrible scream—a scream that carries for miles. It is so piercing, it can shatter glass.

It hurts the heart, however, more than it hurts the ears. A banshee's scream makes a person almost unbearably sad. The banshee, you see, is a messenger of death. Her eyes are red from crying. She grieves for something that is yet to come.

She wails because someone is about to die.

And who is this someone? You can't be sure, but you can make a guess. If several banshees are wailing together, it will be someone great and important. If a banshee is lurking near someone's front door, it will be someone in that house. If the clothes the banshee is washing are your clothes—uh oh! You had better start saying your good-byes.

The Irish have been telling banshee stories for centuries. One such story goes back to 1655. That year, an Irish woman named Lady Fanshawe was staying at the castle of a friend. Many other guests were staying there overnight as well.

Around 1:00 A.M., a sound awoke Lady Fanshawe. She got out of bed. She parted the curtains to look outside. There in the moonlight, she saw a woman dressed in white. The moonlight shone through that woman as if through a cloud. The woman spoke two words aloud. "A horse," she said. Then she let out a sigh so long and loud, it sounded like the wind. Lady Fanshawe was frightened. She felt her hair standing on end. About an hour later, the guest in the next room died. No one knew he was even ill!

Where do banshees come from? The answer goes back to very ancient times. According to the Irish, a different race of beings lived in Ireland before people came. They looked like humans but had certain powers. They could see the future. They were named the *sidhe,* which means "fairies." The sidhe women were known as *bean-sidhe,* or "woman fairies." The English, who came much later, pronounced that name *ban-shee.* Over the years, this turned into *banshee*.

The sidhe were shy folk. When humans arrived, they moved away. They went to live in the hills. They live out there still. No one sees them because they can blend in with any landscape. The sidhe, therefore, are also called the Hill Folk.

Some banshees among these Hill Folk had magical voices. Their songs could stir up any emotion. People had them sing at special occasions. For example, they created joy at weddings. The Hill Folk admired the singing banshees so much, they asked them to rule.

The queen of the banshees now became stuck up. She thought she was better than other Hill Folk. One day, she ordered that twenty of her subjects be killed. The sidhe revolted. They overthrew the queen and her friends. They cast a spell on them. "You wished death upon others," they said. "May death now be all you see." After that, they drove the queen and her friends out of their world.

The banished banshees soon learned the meaning of the curse. They had to spend all their time with people on the verge of death. They were able to express only one emotion with their songs—grief.

It is probably not fair to call banshees monsters. They do no real harm. They do not cause anybody's death. They only see death coming.

But that is exactly why no one wants to see a banshee coming.

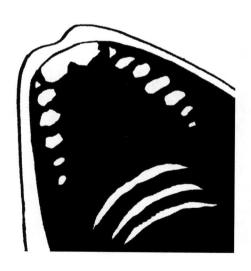

There is a famous story about a detective
named Sherlock Holmes. It tells about
a frightening demon dog. This dog is seen

standing over a dead man, plucking at his throat. It has the shape of a hound but is the size of a small horse. Its jaws drip blood and blaze with a blue fire.

In the story, this monster turns out to be a fake. It is just a big dog. The blue fire is a special effect. Some crook has been using the dog to cover up his crimes. But don't relax just yet. The writer based this creature on stories he had heard about demon dogs. And such stories go way back.

Around the year 800 C.E., for example, a huge black dog prowled the dark woods of Germany. It was tearing people to pieces. A German lord named Frankenstein killed the thing. (He was not related to the Frankenstein of the monster stories.) In the battle, Frankenstein got a small scratch. That tiny scratch ended up killing the poor man.

Was he scratched by a dog with rabies? Rabies is a fearful disease carried by dogs and other mammals. It makes dogs act crazy: That's why dogs with rabies are called "mad dogs." Even a scratch from such a dog can pass on the illness. And in the old days, there was no cure for rabies. Almost everyone who got the illness died.

But why was that dog so huge? Perhaps it was not a dog after all. Perhaps it was a wolf. A black wolf with rabies— that would be very scary, demon or not.

There are other stories. In 1874, something started killing sheep in Ireland. It killed about 30 sheep a night. This thing did not eat the sheep. It just sucked out their blood through small cuts in their throats. The tracks of an enormous dog were found in the area. The creature itself was never seen. After a while, the killings just ended.

Then in 1905, the same kind of killings started up in Badminton, England.

Demon Dogs

This time, farmers got together. They went out looking for a demon dog. They shot all the stray dogs they could find. It didn't help. Those stray dogs were not doing any harm. The killings were the work of some other creature. What creature? Experts said it could not be a dog. Dogs are not vampires; they do not suck blood. Dogs eat meat. Yet this creature was eating none of the meat of the sheep it killed. It was just sucking them dry of blood.

This story has happened many times in many places. The pattern is always the same. Something starts killing sheep or cattle. The attacks go on for many nights. The animals are not eaten, but their blood is sucked out. The footprints of a giant dog are found near the killings. People look for the giant dog but find no trace of it. Then the killings stop, leaving people to wonder. What was that creature? Where did it come from? Where did it go?

The mystery has given rise to stories about werewolves. These are people who can change their shape. They look human most of the time. But on some nights they turn into wolflike creatures. Then they go out thirsty for blood. After they have killed enough animals and drunk enough blood, they change back to human shape. That's why they are never found.

Stories about wolf men don't just come from long ago. New reports keep turning up. It's hard to know what to make of a story from Lawton, Texas, for example. It was printed on December 27, 1971. According to this story, a police officer named Harry Ezell took almost 100 calls one night. The callers said that "something" was running down their streets. It was dodging between cars. It was hiding behind bushes, then leaping out to run again. It was scaring people.

Demon Dogs

Many callers described this creature as a "wolf man." They said it had hair over its whole face. They said it had hair on its hands and lower legs, too. It was wearing clothes, but the pants were too small. They were torn in some places. It looked as if the creature had grown since it put on those clothes.

A man named Donald Childs had a heart attack when he saw the wolf man in his yard. It was on its hands and knees, drinking from his fishpond. The thing stood up and turned. Childs saw that it was tall and had hair over its whole face. He felt faint. When he woke up, he was in the hospital.

A woman saw the thing on her second-story balcony. She had no idea how it got up there. When she looked out, it jumped down. The ground was 17 feet down, but the creature landed with no problem.

"Something" was in Lawton that night, but what was it? We will never know. And most of us would rather not find out.